Reflections
A CHILD'S VIEW

CALIFORNIA

S.O.S.

Spotlight on Standards Reader

Harcourt
SCHOOL PUBLISHERS

Orlando   Austin   New York   San Diego   Toronto   London
Visit *The Learning Site!* **www.harcourtschool.com**

MAPQUEST®   TIME® FOR KIDS

Printed in the United States of America

ISBN 0-15-348998-7

4 5 6 7 8 9 10 030 11 10 09 08 07 06

i

Contents

Unit 1

Rules and Laws

The Big Idea

California Standards

HSS 1.1

iv

Rules and laws help people.

Good citizens follow rules
and laws.

Vocabulary

community A group of people who live and work together. It is also the place where they live.

citizen A person who lives in and belongs to a community.

rule   An instruction that tells people how to act.

law   A rule that people in a community must follow.

vote   A choice that gets counted.

INTERNET RESOURCES

Go to **www.harcourtschool.com/hss** to view Internet resources for this unit.

3

School Rules

The teacher is the leader of the class.

This is our **teacher**.

She helps make the **rules**.

The principal is the leader of the school.

This is our **principal**. He makes rules for the school. One rule is to be **fair**.

We must follow all rules.
Following rules is a **responsibility**.

Activity

Make a Class Rule Poster

Step 1 Think about a class rule.

Step 2 Write it on your paper.

Step 3 Draw a picture for the rule.

Step 4 Share your poster with your classmates.

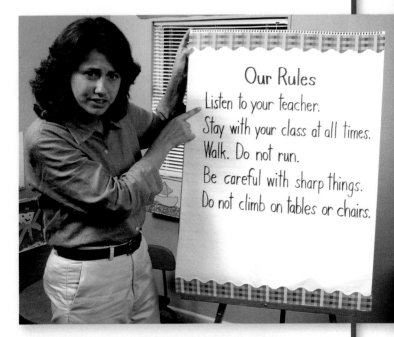

Community Rules

This is my **community**. People here live and work together.

Huntington Beach, California

Communities have rules called **laws**.
People in a community must follow laws.

Police officers help people follow laws.

Laws help us live together and be safe.

Activity

Make a Police Hat and Badge

Step 1 Trace and cut out the parts to make a hat.

Step 2 Staple or glue them together.

Step 3 Trace and cut out your badge. Use crayons to decorate it.

Step 4 Imagine that you are a police officer. Talk about your work.

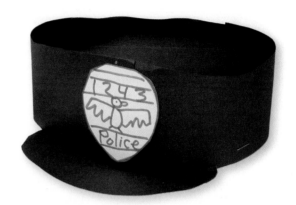

Our Leaders

Yim Kwan is a community **leader**.

Yim Kwan is our **mayor**. A mayor is
the leader of a **city**.

Mayor Kwan leads the city **government**.
The government is a group of people
who lead our community.

Activity

Make a Community Leader Puppet

Step 1 Think about your teacher, your principal, a coach, or the mayor. Choose one community leader.

Step 2 Draw and cut out a picture of the leader.

Step 3 Glue a craft stick to the back of your cutout.

Step 4 Have your puppet tell a partner about his or her work.

The Golden Rule

The Golden Rule says to be fair to people.
I am fair at school and at home.

I treat others fairly.

The Golden Rule helps me **respect** others.

In the United States,
people have the right
to talk about things that
are important to them.

We should show respect to others.
We should respect their **rights**.

Activity
Make a Golden Rule Book

Step 1 Make a small book about the Golden Rule.

Step 2 Write about three ways you follow the Golden Rule.

Step 3 Illustrate your book.

The Golden Rule Book

Wrap-Up

 Review **The Big Idea**

Look at the cause-and-effect chart.
Then answer the questions.

cause	effect
People follow rules and laws.	**People live together safely.**

Why should people follow rules and laws?
What could happen if they don't?

Review **Vocabulary**

1. Give an example of playing **fair**.
2. Name a **leader** in your **community**.
3. What is a **government**?

Show What You Know

Copy the chart.

- In the first box, name and draw a leader in your community.
- In the other boxes write or draw three things he or she does.

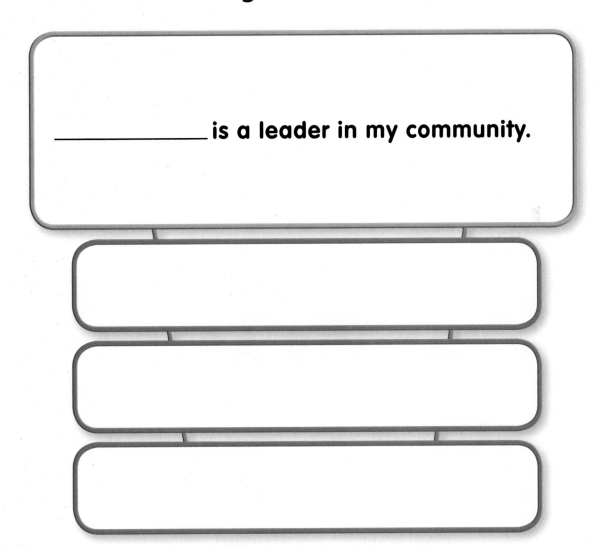

_____ is a leader in my community.

Unit 2

Where People Live

The Big Idea

California Standards
HSS 1.2

We live in the state of California.

San Francisco, California

People in different places
live in different ways.

Vocabulary

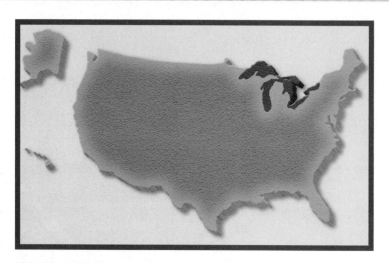

country   An area of land with its own people and laws.

state   A part of a country.

globe A model of Earth.

continent A large area of land.

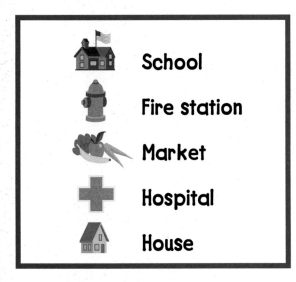

School

Fire station

Market

Hospital

House

symbol A picture or an object that stands for something.

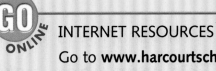

INTERNET RESOURCES
Go to **www.harcourtschool.com/hss**
to view Internet resources for this unit.

Finding Where You Are

A **map** shows the **locations** of places. This map shows streets and places in a community.

On this map, green shows land and blue shows water.

California

Sacramento ★

San Francisco

•San Jose

PACIFIC OCEAN

•Los Angeles

San Diego

Eureka

Redding

Santa Rosa

★ Sacramento

San Francisco

•San Jose

•Fresno

Monterey

Bakersfield

Barstow

Lompoc

Los Angeles

San Diego

This map shows the locations of cities in the state of California.

There are many kinds of maps. Maps can show cities. They can show oceans and rivers, too.

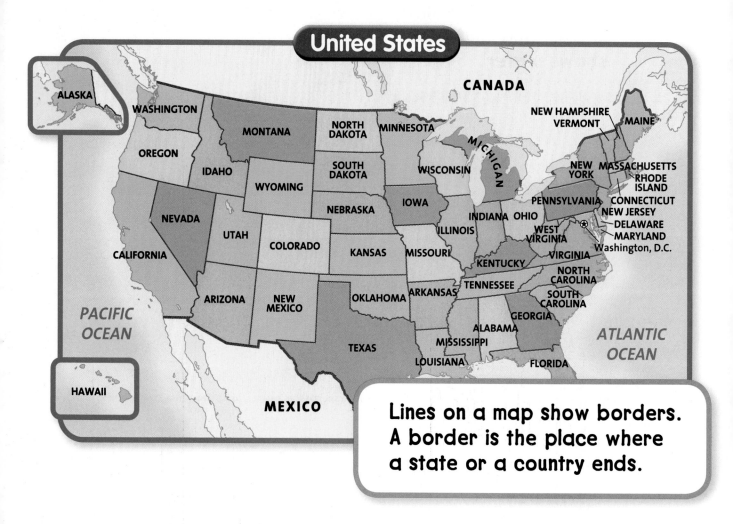

United States

CANADA

ALASKA

WASHINGTON

OREGON

IDAHO

MONTANA

NORTH DAKOTA

SOUTH DAKOTA

WYOMING

NEVADA

UTAH

COLORADO

CALIFORNIA

ARIZONA

NEW MEXICO

MINNESOTA

WISCONSIN

MICHIGAN

IOWA

NEBRASKA

KANSAS

OKLAHOMA

TEXAS

MISSOURI

ARKANSAS

LOUISIANA

ILLINOIS

INDIANA

OHIO

KENTUCKY

TENNESSEE

MISSISSIPPI

ALABAMA

GEORGIA

NEW HAMPSHIRE

VERMONT

MAINE

NEW YORK

MASSACHUSETTS

RHODE ISLAND

CONNECTICUT

NEW JERSEY

DELAWARE

MARYLAND

Washington, D.C.

PENNSYLVANIA

WEST VIRGINIA

VIRGINIA

NORTH CAROLINA

SOUTH CAROLINA

FLORIDA

PACIFIC OCEAN

HAWAII

MEXICO

ATLANTIC OCEAN

Lines on a map show borders. A border is the place where a state or a country ends.

This map shows the location of the United States. It is our **country**. Canada and Mexico are also countries.

28

Activity

Trace a Map of California

Step 1 Look at a map of the United States. Find the state of California.

CALIFORNIA

Step 2 Trace the outline of your state.

Step 3 Look at the shape of the state. Then draw California on your own.

Step 4 Make a mark to show the location of your community.

Barstow

Neighborhood Map

Kim and her dad walked around their
neighborhood. They used a map to
find her new school.

Kim took pictures of places she saw.
The map and Kim's pictures show the
same places.

A model is another way to show a place.

Then Kim made a model
of her neighborhood.

Activity
Make a Neighborhood Model

Step 1 Make a list of places in your neighborhood. Choose one building to make.

Step 2 Choose a box that is shaped like your building. Paint it with one color.

Step 3 Add details to your box. Draw windows, a door, and the name of the building.

Step 4 Add your finished building to the others from your group.

The Land Around You

There are many kinds of land in California.
Each kind of land has **resources**.

sheep

almonds

fish

Soil, trees, and water are resources.
People use the resources that come from
where they live.

Imperial Valley, California

The food you eat comes from **farms** across the country.

Activity

Make a Community Booklet

Tell about your community's location and its resources.

Step 1 Fold your paper into three parts.

Step 2 On the first part, write your title. Use crayons or markers to decorate it.

Step 3 On the second part, draw a picture of your neighborhood.

Step 4 On the third part, draw and label the resources found near your community.

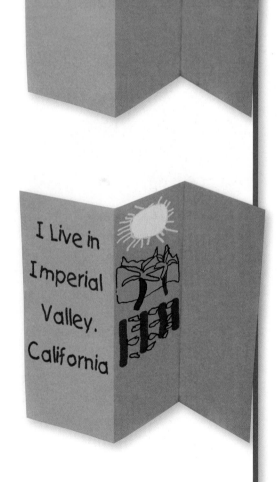

I Live in Imperial Valley, California

4

What's the Weather?

California has many kinds of **weather**.
Weather is the way the air feels outside.

Spring

Summer

Fall

Winter

There are four seasons in a year.
The weather changes every season.

People choose clothes that will keep them warm, dry, or cool.

People look at the weather to decide what to wear. It also helps them decide what to do for fun.

Activity

Make a Clothing Poster

Think about the clothes you wear when the weather is hot and and when it is cold.

Step 1 On the left side of your poster, draw yourself wearing clothes for a hot day.

Step 2 On the right side, draw yourself wearing clothes for a cold day.

Step 3 Label your pictures. Share your poster with a partner.

Wrap-Up

💡 Review **The Big Idea**

Look at the diagram. Then follow the directions.

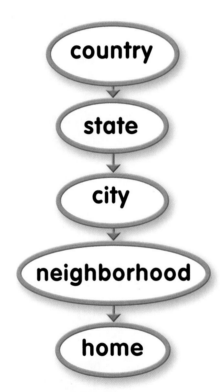

country
↓
state
↓
city
↓
neighborhood
↓
home

Describe each location named in the diagram.

Review **Vocabulary**

1. How is a **model** different from a **map**?

2. What **country** do you live in?

3. Describe today's **weather** where you live.

 Copy the chart. Write **yes** or **no** in the spaces to tell whether that resource is found near your community. Then write a sentence about the resources where you live.

Resources	
water	
trees	
soil	

We Love
Our Country

The Big Idea

California
Standards

HSS 1.3

Our country has many symbols,
heroes, and holidays.

Some symbols stand for people and places. Others stand for events.

Vocabulary

flag   A piece of cloth with colors and shapes that stand for things.

hero   A person who does something brave or important to help others.

landmark   A symbol that is a place people can visit.

national holiday   A day to honor a person or an event that is important to our country.

freedom   The right people have to make their own choices.

GO ONLINE

INTERNET RESOURCES

Go to **www.harcourtschool.com/hss** to view Internet resources for this unit.

I Pledge Allegiance

The American **flag** is a symbol.

48

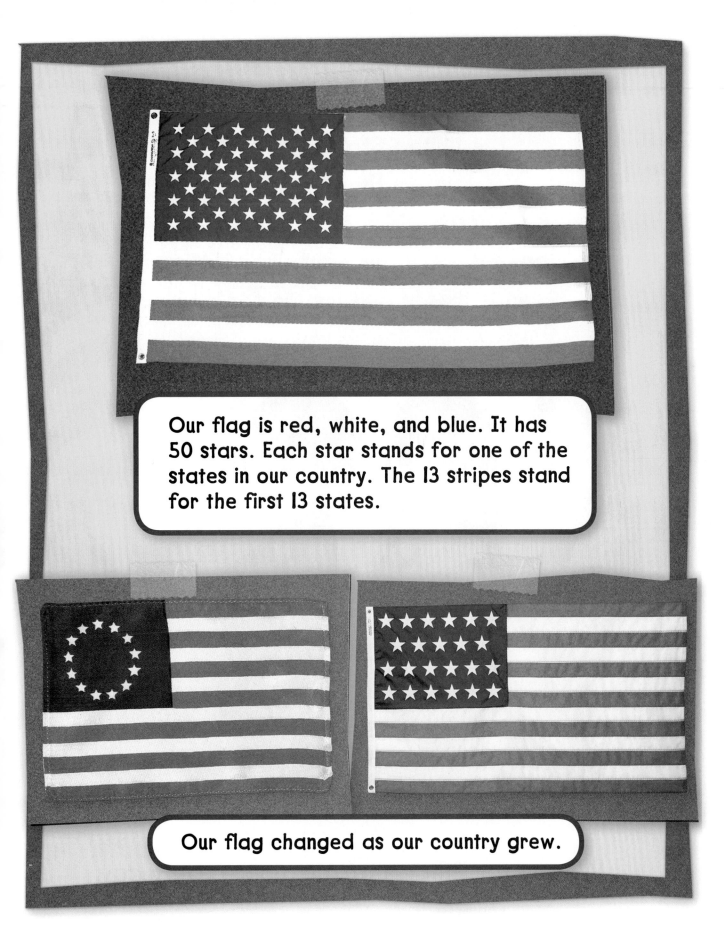

Our flag is red, white, and blue. It has 50 stars. Each star stands for one of the states in our country. The 13 stripes stand for the first 13 states.

Our flag changed as our country grew.

The Pledge of Allegiance

I pledge allegiance to the Flag
of the United States of America,
and to the Republic
for which it stands,
one Nation under God, indivisible,
with liberty and justice for all.

We say the **Pledge** of Allegiance every day.

Activity

Paint the United States Flag

Step 1 Draw the outline of the flag.

Step 2 Paint the flag. Use red, white, and blue.

Step 3 When your flag is dry, display it in your classroom.

Step 4 Look at your flag and say the Pledge of Allegiance.

Heroes and Holidays

Men and women in the military are **heroes**. They keep us safe.

On Memorial Day and Veterans Day, we remember the people who help our country in wars.

We thank our heroes on **national holidays**. Memorial Day and Veterans Day are national holidays.

We do special things on national holidays.
We have parades. Our families get together.

Activity

Make a Kazoo

Step 1 Use crayons to decorate a paper-towel tube.

Step 2 Attach wax paper to the end of the tube with a rubber band.

Step 3 Hum gently into the open end of the tube.

Step 4 Have a holiday parade. Hum "The Star Spangled Banner" into your kazoo.

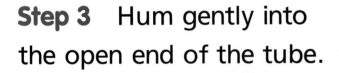

American Symbols

Liberty Bell

Our country has many symbols. Some symbols are plants or animals. The rose is an American symbol. So is the bald eagle.

Bald Eagle

Symbols help us think of special things about our country.

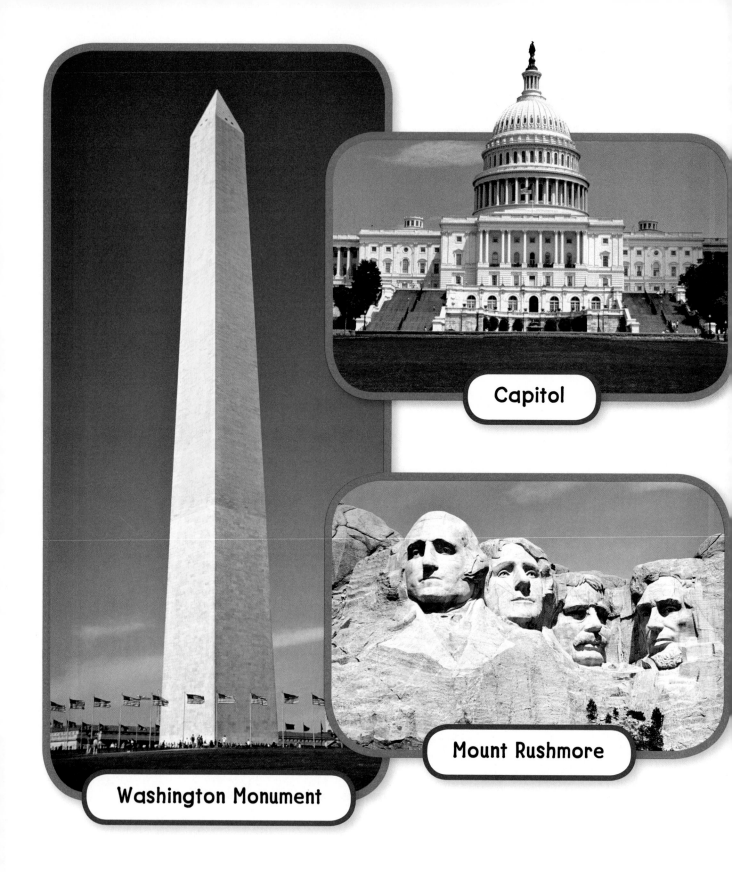

Capitol

Mount Rushmore

Washington Monument

Some symbols are places. These symbols are
called **landmarks**.

Activity

Make Shape Symbols

Step 1   Use pattern blocks to make the shape of a national symbol.

Step 2   Use paper shapes to make the symbol again.

Step 3   Glue the paper shapes onto a sheet of paper.

Step 4   Label your symbol, and share it with others.

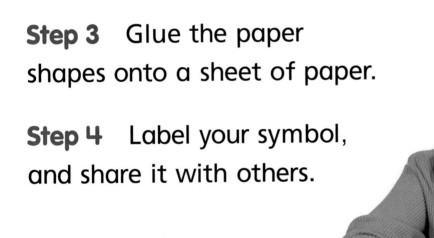

Lesson 4

Our Country Begins

Long ago, **settlers** came to North America. Many settlers were from England.

60

The king of England called their land a **colony**.
The land was ruled by England. The settlers
were not happy.

On July 4, 1776, the Declaration of Independence told England that Americans wanted to be free. Today, July 4 is celebrated as Independence Day.

They did not like England's rules. They went to war with England. They won their **freedom**.

Activity
Make a Settler's Suitcase

Step 1 Fold a sheet of construction paper in half. Attach a handle to the top to make a suitcase.

Step 2 Pretend you are a settler going to North America. Think about what you would take with you.

Step 3 Open your suitcase. Draw three things you would take to the colonies.

Step 4 Compare your suitcase with a partner's suitcase.

Wrap-Up

 Review **The Big Idea**

Look at the word web. Then answer the questions.

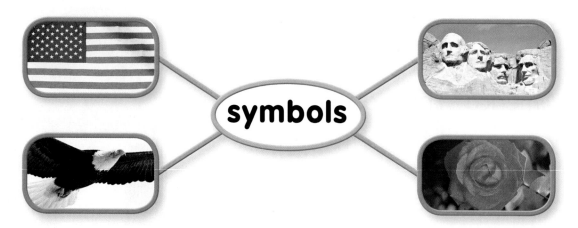

symbols

How are American symbols the same? How are they different?

Review **Vocabulary**

1. Say the **Pledge** of Allegiance to the person sitting next to you.

2. What makes a person a **hero**? Name a hero.

3. Why do Americans celebrate Indepencence Day?

Show What You Know

Copy the chart. Draw some things you and your family do to celebrate this holiday. Write a sentence about the best part of the day.

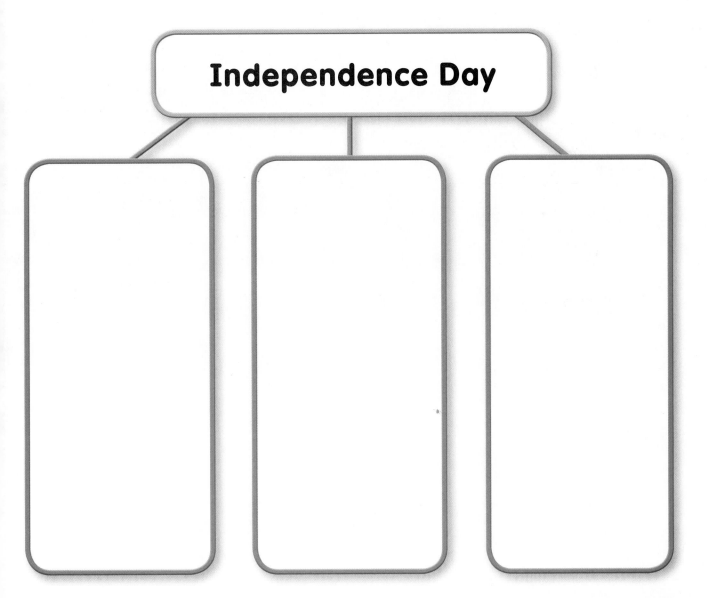

Independence Day

Unit 4
Our Changing World

The Big Idea

California Standards
HSS 1.4

66

Today people are a lot like they were long ago.

The way people live has
changed over time.

Vocabulary

past The time before now.

present The time now.

change To become different.

technology All of the tools we use to make our lives easier.

0   1   2   3   4

time line A line that shows the order in which things have happened.

GO **ONLINE**

INTERNET RESOURCES

Go to **www.harcourtschool.com/hss** to view Internet resources for this unit.

Schools Long Ago

One-room school, 1917

Long ago, schools had one room.
All children had the same teacher.
Children used different **tools** to learn.

Special-needs school

Public school

Home school

Today, children go to many kinds of
schools. Most schools have many rooms.
There is also more than one teacher.

Many things have **changed** in schools.
Some things have stayed the same.

Activity

Make Your Own Slate

Step 1 Trace a large rectangle on brown construction paper. Cut it out to make a frame.

Step 2 Place black construction paper behind the frame. Tape it to the frame.

Step 3 Write your name on your slate. Use chalk.

Joshua

Communities in the Past

Past

Marc lives in Julian, California.
This was his community in the **past**.

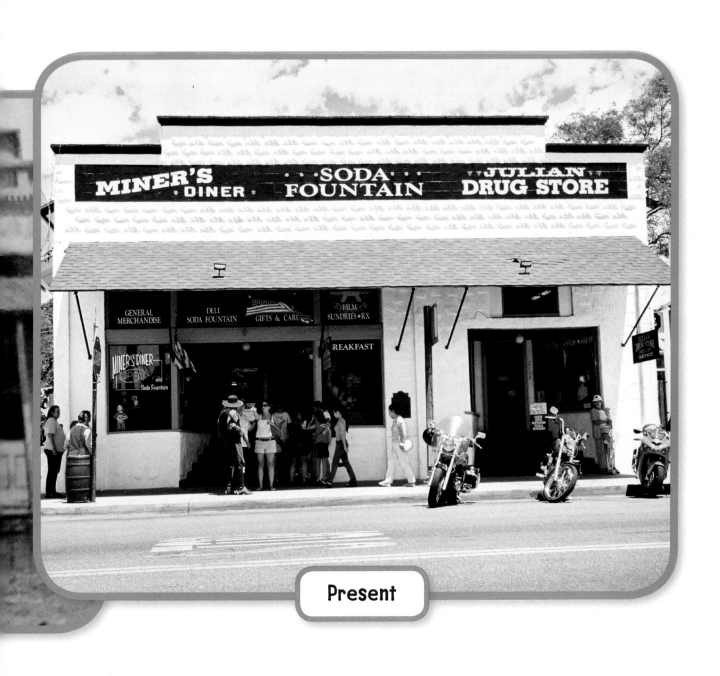

Present

This is Marc's community in the **present**.

Work can change in a community.
People used to look for gold in Julian.
Now they grow apples.

Draw a Worker of the Present

Step 1 Draw a picture of a worker in your community. Label the picture.

Step 2 Outline the drawing with glue. Let it dry.

Step 3 Paint around the outside of your glue border.

Changes in Transportation

Lesson **3**

Transportation used to be slow. It took a long time for people to go places.

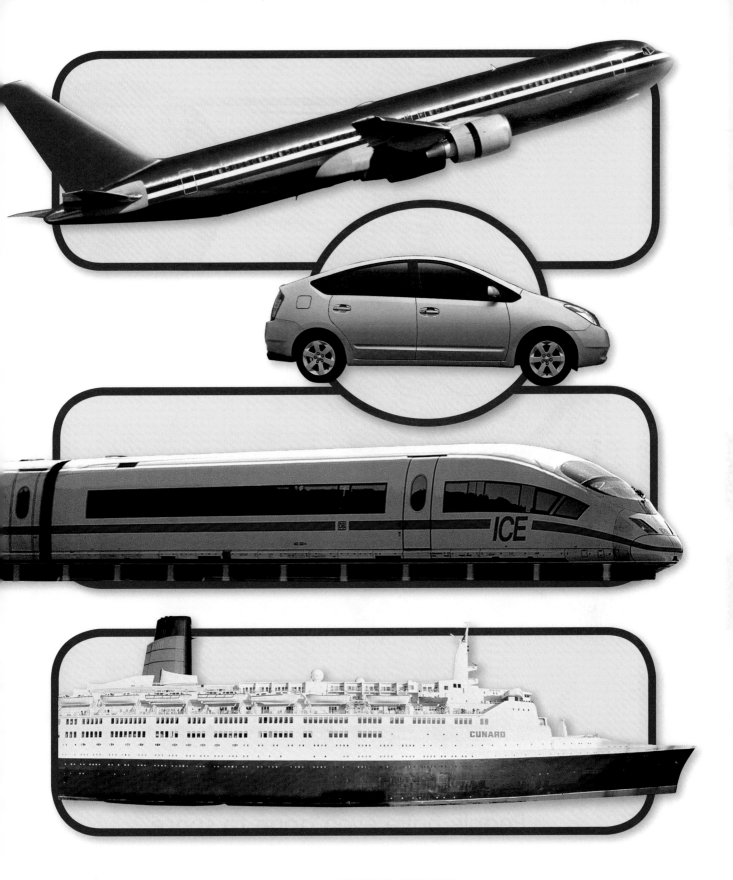

People used **technology** to make transportation safe and fast.

People have even gone to space.

Activity

Make a Transportation Mobile

Step 1 Gather the materials you see in the picture.

Step 2 Draw a picture of a form of transportation on each circle.

Step 3 Attach string to each circle. Then tie the string onto the hanger.

Step 4 Hang your mobile. Tell about the different forms of transportation.

People in the Past

Grandma Mary has pictures of when she was a girl. Many things have changed.

Some things people do have stayed the same over time. Other things people do have changed.

Grandma Mary's mother worked at home.
Grandma Mary works as a dentist.

People talk and write to share ideas and feelings. This sharing is called communication.

You Have Mail!

In the past, Grandma Mary wrote letters. Sometimes she called on the phone. Today she can send letters on a computer.

Step 1 Draw pictures of yourself living in the past. Show your clothes. Show your toys.

Step 2 Glue or tape each picture onto a separate sheet of paper. Label each picture.

Step 3 Use markers and crayons to decorate the cover of your album.

Wrap-Up

Review **The Big Idea**

Look at the chart. Then answer the question.

Communication	
Same as Past	**Different from Past**
writing letters	using e-mail
talking on the phone	talking on cell phones

How do you communicate with people?

Review **Vocabulary**

1. Tell about a game that was played in the **past** and is still played in the **present**.

2. How has your neighborhood **changed** over time?

Show What You Know

 Copy the chart.

• Draw a picture of a car of the past.

• Next, draw a car used today.

• Last, draw a car of the future.

• Write a sentence to describe your cars.

Past	Present	Future

Unit 5

All About People

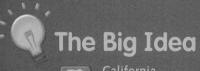

The Big Idea

California Standards
HSS 1.5

88

Americans come from many cultures.

聯合銀行

951

Chinatown,
Los Angeles, CA

We learn about cultures
from our neighbors.

Vocabulary

culture   A group's way of life.

tradition   A special way of doing something that is passed on from families to children.

history The story of what happened in the past.

immigrant A person from another part of the world who has come to live in this country.

custom A group's way of doing something.

INTERNET RESOURCES
Go to **www.harcourtschool.com/hss** to view Internet resources for this unit.

People Together

A community is made up of many **cultures**.

Clothes, foods, and dances teach us
about cultures.

Learning about **traditions** helps us get along.

Activity

Make a Culture Mobile

Step 1 Glue a picture of yourself to a large circle.

Step 2 Bring pictures from home that show your family's culture.

Step 3 Glue each picture to a smaller circle. Hang the small circles from the larger one.

Step 4 Compare your mobile to others.

2

America's First People

Nez Perce

Mandan

Pomo

Hopi

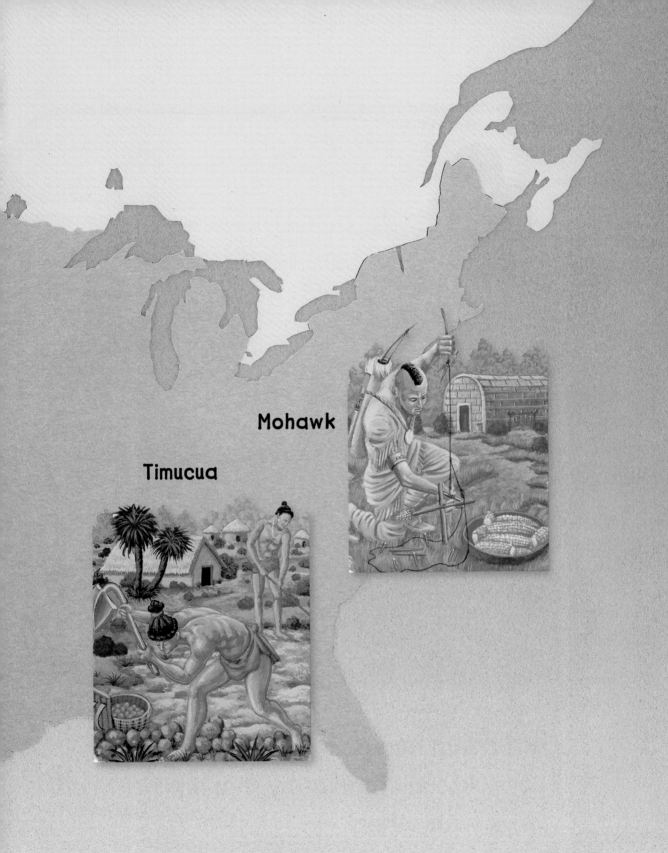

Mohawk

Timucua

American Indians lived in our country first.
There were many different groups.

Each group had its own **language**.
They told their **history** by sharing
stories with others.

Weave a Place Mat

Some American Indians were basket weavers. Share your culture with a weaving.

Step 1 Weave paper strips in and out of a sheet of cut paper.

Step 2 Cut a shape into a folded sheet of paper.

Step 3 Glue the border onto the weave. Add designs with a crayon.

People Find New Homes

Kwame is from Ghana.

Anahat is from India.

Anahat, Kwame, Juan, and Yana are **immigrants**. Their families have moved to the United States from another country.

100

Juan is from El Salvador.

Yana is from Russia.

Immigrants share their **cultures**.

Immigrants have come to the United States for many years. They are still coming.

Activity

Design a Family Flag

Make a flag to represent your family.

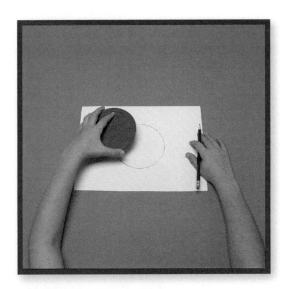

Step 1 Think of ideas about your family for your flag.

Step 2 Draw your design. You can trace objects to make shapes you need.

Step 3 Paint your design. Then glue one side of your flag to a craft stick.

Step 4 Hold up your family flag and explain it to the class.

Lesson 4

Expressing Culture

Every culture has folktales. A **folktale** is a story passed from person to person.

Mexican puppets

Hawaiian dancers

Folktales tell about people and places.
They can also tell about traditions.

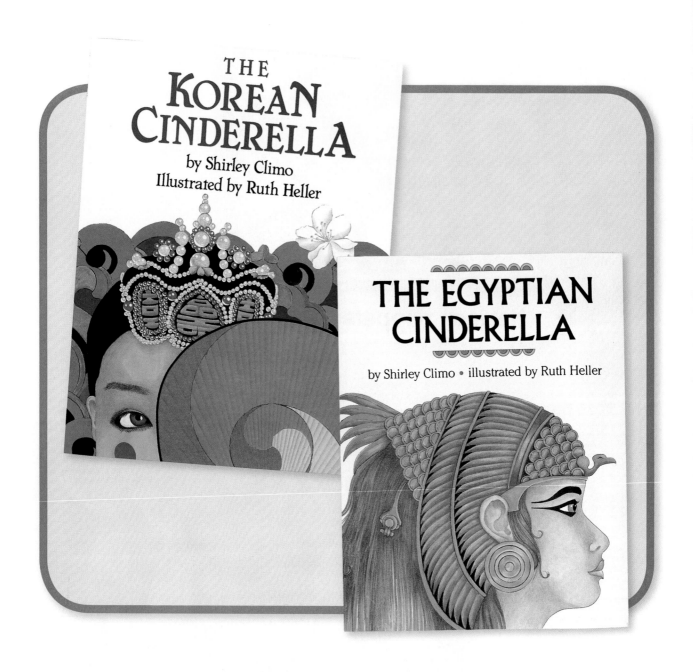

Some folktales can be found in many cultures. They are the same story told in different ways.

Activity

Make a Character Mask

Step 1 Choose a character in a folktale.

Step 2 Trace and cut out the head shape. Then cut out the eye holes.

Step 3 Add details to your mask. Use paper, yarn, or ribbon to make hair.

Step 4 Put on your mask. See if your classmates can guess who you are!

Sharing Cultures

Li's family celebrates the Chinese New Year. Li learns about Chinese **celebrations** from his family.

Anita celebrates Cinco de Mayo. It is an important holiday in Mexico. Anita's family teaches her about Mexican culture.

People in our country celebrate many special days. Celebrations helps us learn about one another.

Activity

Make a Chinese New Year Dragon

Step 1 Staple the ends of a paper strip together to make a circle. Link another strip through the circle and staple it.

Step 2 Make a chain by adding more links. Stop when you have 10 links.

Step 3 Make a head for your dragon. Attach it to the paper chain.

Step 4 Have a dragon parade with your classmates!

Wrap-Up

Review **The Big Idea**

Look at the word web. Then answer the question.

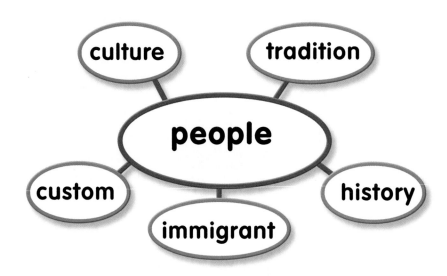

How are people in a community the same and different?

Review **Vocabulary**

1. How does your family remember its **history**?

2. What is a **custom**?

3. Name one of your family **celebrations**.

Show What You Know

 Copy the web. Then draw pictures or write words to tell about your traditions.

What We Eat

What We Wear

Traditions

What We Do

Unit 6

The Marketplace

The Big Idea

California Standards

HSS 1.6

People trade goods and services.

People decide how to spend
their money.

Vocabulary

goods   Things that people make or grow or sell.

services   Kinds of work people do for others for money.

trade To give one thing to get another thing.

factory A building in which people use machines to make goods.

market A place where people buy and sell goods.

INTERNET RESOURCES

Go to **www.harcourtschool.com/hss** to view Internet resources for this unit.

117

Goods and Services

Communities have many kinds of workers. Some workers make goods. **Goods** are things that people make or grow to sell.

118

Some workers sell goods. People can buy goods in stores.

Veterinarian

Mail carrier

Bus driver

Some workers sell **services**. We use many kinds of services. People use **money** to pay for goods and services.

120

Activity

Make Goods to Sell

Step 1 Think of some things you could make to sell.

Step 2 Use modeling clay to make the objects.

Step 3 Put each object on an index card. Label the obects and write their prices.

Step 4 Set out your goods in a class store.

Jobs People Do

Mrs. Brown has a job. A **job** is work that people do to earn money.

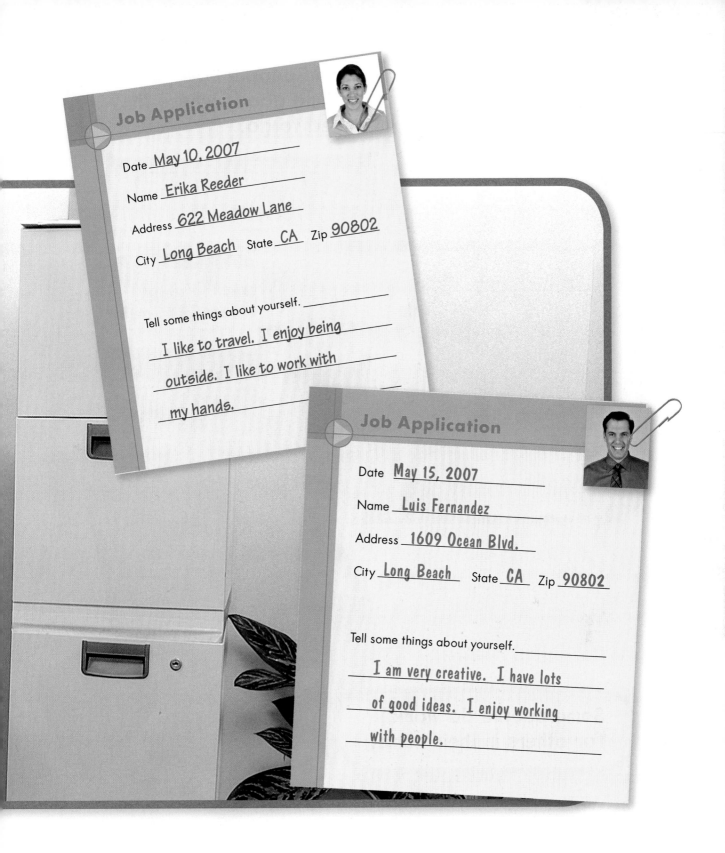

Job Application

Date May 10, 2007

Name Erika Reeder

Address 622 Meadow Lane

City Long Beach State CA Zip 90802

Tell some things about yourself.
I like to travel. I enjoy being
outside. I like to work with
my hands.

Job Application

Date May 15, 2007

Name Luis Fernandez

Address 1609 Ocean Blvd.

City Long Beach State CA Zip 90802

Tell some things about yourself.
I am very creative. I have lots
of good ideas. I enjoy working
with people.

Mrs. Brown owns a **business**. She helps
people find jobs.

Some people have jobs taking goods where they need to go.

Some people do work for others in their home.

People do many kinds of jobs. They work to earn money.

Activity

Make a Job Puzzle

Step 1 Draw a picture of yourself doing a job you want to have when you are older.

Step 2 Cut your picture into six large pieces. Put them into an envelope.

Step 3 Trade puzzles with a partner. Put your partner's puzzle together.

Step 4 Talk with your partner about the job.

Buyers and Sellers

Amy's community has a **market**. Amy has money to spend. She wants to buy a gift.

Amy will **trade** some of her money to get the gift.

"A penny saved
is a penny earned."

—Benjamin Franklin

from *Poor Richard's Almanack*, 1737

Amy does not spend all of her money.
She **saves** some of it.

Activity

Make A Money Bank

Step 1 Paint the outside of a container with one color.

Step 2 Use markers and crayons to decorate your bank.

Step 3 Cut an opening in the top of the container to drop in your money.

Step 4 Talk about what you want to save your money for.

4 Working in a Factory

Did you ever wonder how crayons are made? Crayons are made in a **factory**.

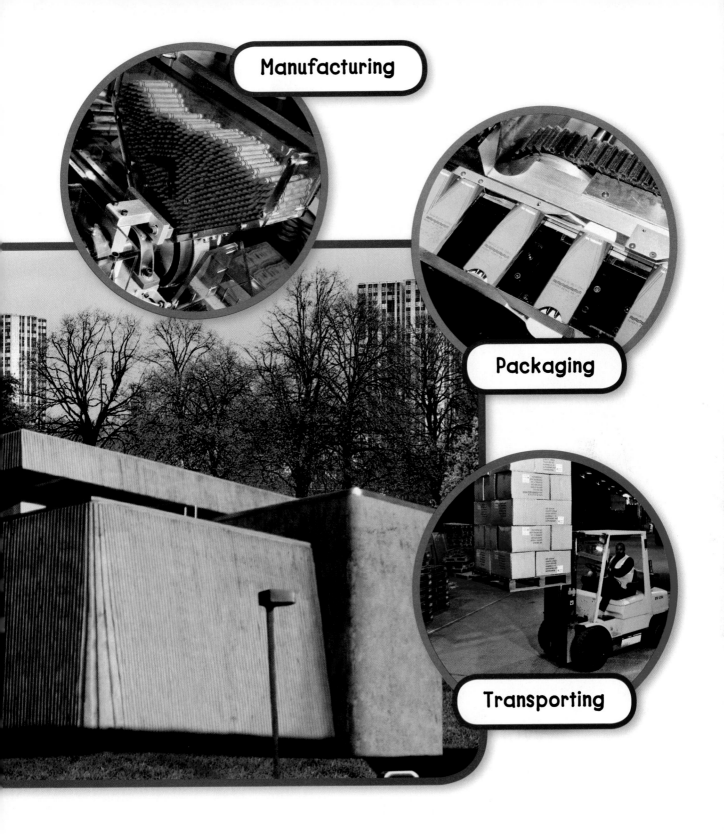

Manufacturing

Packaging

Transporting

Different workers do different jobs.
After the crayons are made, they are
sent to stores.

Workers use machines to put
the crayons in boxes.

Workers in stores sell the crayons.
The crayons you use in school
came from a factory.

Activity

Make a Silly Creature

Work with two classmates to make a group drawing.

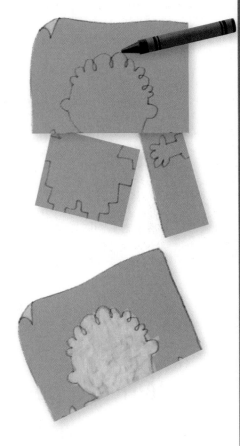

Step 1 Draw the outline of a body. Cut the paper into the head, the body, arms, and the legs and feet.

Step 2 Have each person in your group color one of the body parts.

Step 3 Then put together your silly creature. Share it with the class.

Step 4 Talk about why it is helpful and fun to work with a group.

Wrap-Up

💡 Review **The Big Idea**

Talk about kinds of goods and services. Then answer the question.

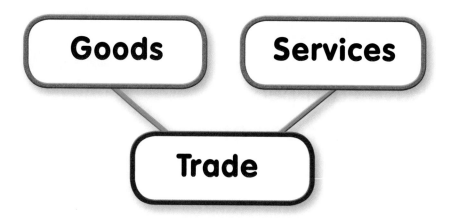

Goods   Services

Trade

Why do people need to trade goods and services?

Review **Vocabulary**

1. How are a **factory** and a **market** different?

2. Why do people have **jobs**?

3. Name a business in your **community**.

Show What You Know

 Copy the chart. Draw pictures of three people you know doing their jobs. Write about the job you would like to have when you are older.

Jobs People Do

Name	Jobs

Atlas

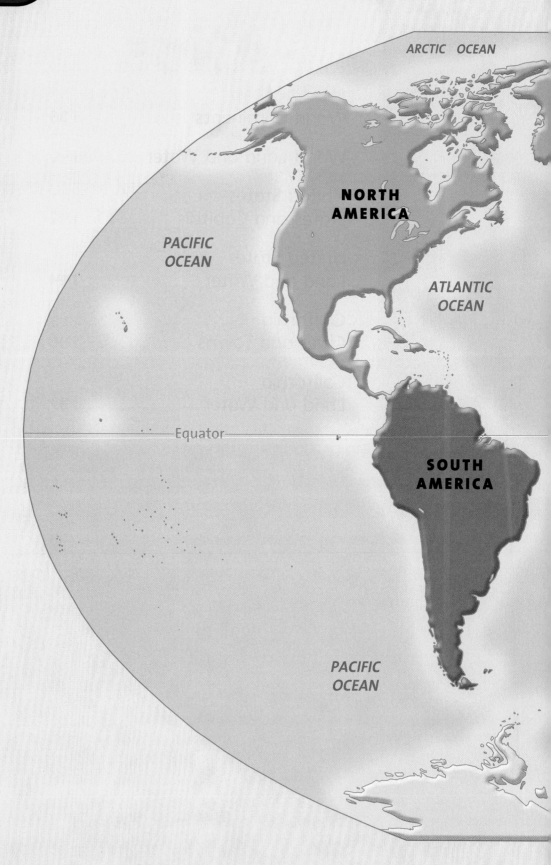

ARCTIC OCEAN

NORTH AMERICA

PACIFIC OCEAN

ATLANTIC OCEAN

Equator

SOUTH AMERICA

PACIFIC OCEAN

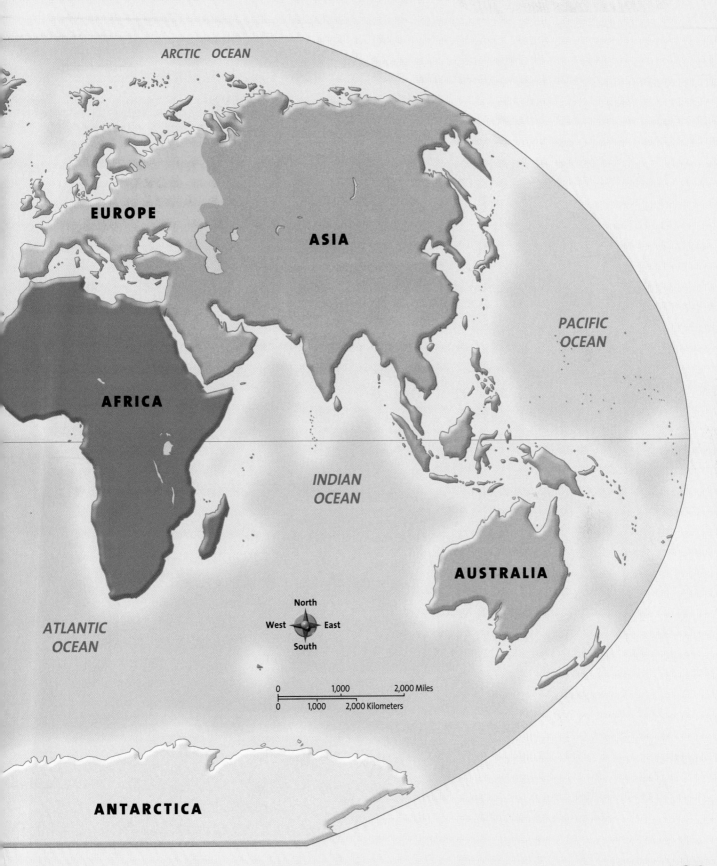

ARCTIC OCEAN

EUROPE

ASIA

AFRICA

PACIFIC OCEAN

INDIAN OCEAN

AUSTRALIA

ATLANTIC OCEAN

North

West ✦ East

South

ANTARCTICA

0   1,000   2,000 Miles

0   1,000   2,000 Kilometers

139

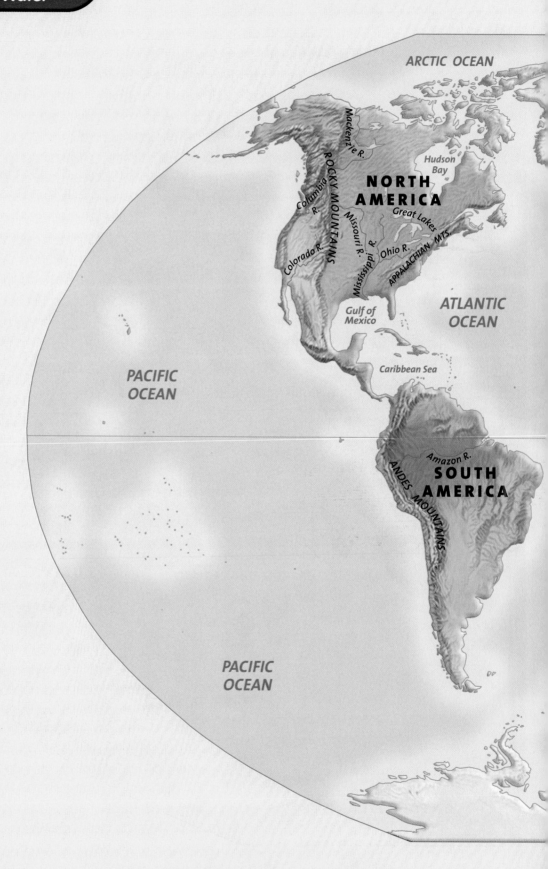

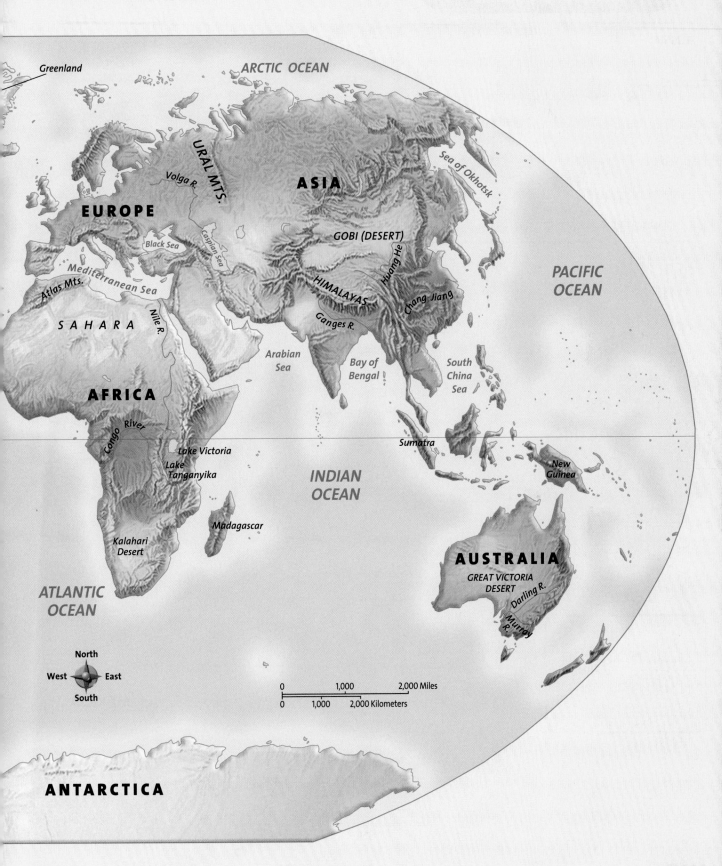

Greenland

ARCTIC OCEAN

EUROPE

URAL MTS.

Volga R.

ASIA

Sea of Okhotsk

Black Sea

Caspian Sea

GOBI (DESERT)

Atlas Mts.

Mediterranean Sea

Huang He

SAHARA

HIMALAYAS

Nile R.

Chang Jiang

PACIFIC OCEAN

Ganges R.

Arabian Sea

AFRICA

Bay of Bengal

South China Sea

Congo River

Lake Victoria

Lake Tanganyika

Sumatra

New Guinea

INDIAN OCEAN

Madagascar

Kalahari Desert

AUSTRALIA

ATLANTIC OCEAN

GREAT VICTORIA DESERT

Darling R.

Murray R.

North

West   East

South

0   1,000   2,000 Miles

0   1,000   2,000 Kilometers

ANTARCTICA

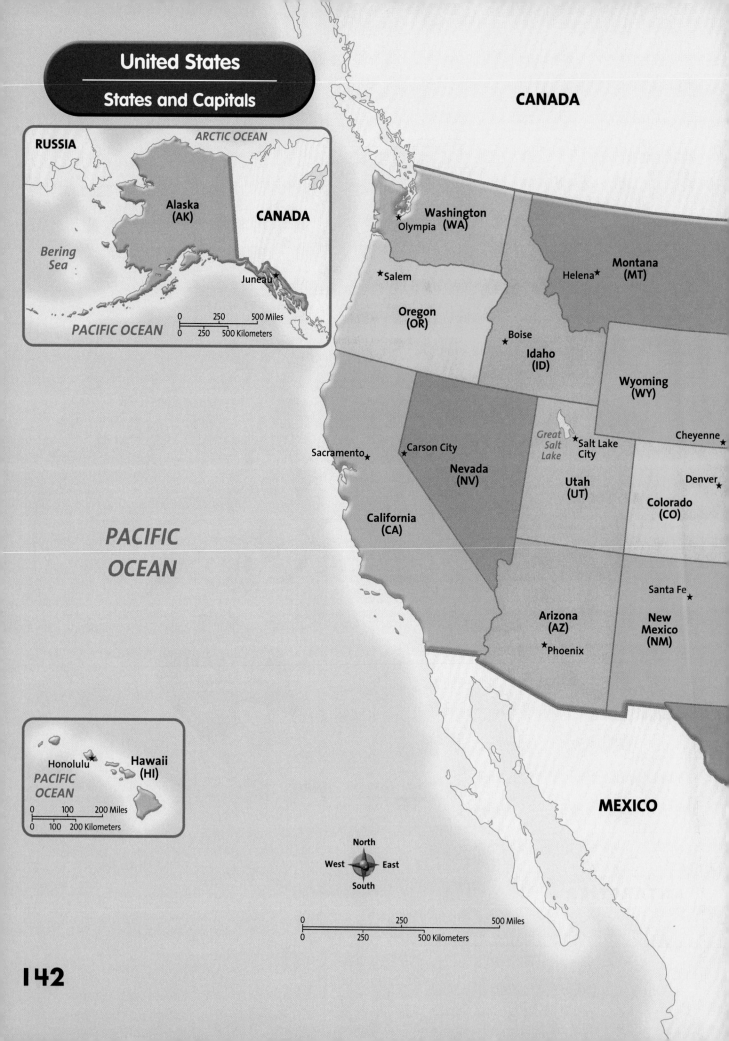

United States

States and Capitals

RUSSIA

ARCTIC OCEAN

Alaska
(AK)

CANADA

*Bering
Sea*

Juneau ★

PACIFIC OCEAN

| 0 | 250 | 500 Miles |
| 0 | 250 | 500 Kilometers |

CANADA

★ Olympia
Washington
(WA)

★ Salem

Oregon
(OR)

Helena ★
Montana
(MT)

★ Boise
Idaho
(ID)

Wyoming
(WY)

*Great
Salt
Lake*
★ Salt Lake
City

Cheyenne ★

Sacramento ★
★ Carson City

Nevada
(NV)

Utah
(UT)

Denver ★

Colorado
(CO)

California
(CA)

PACIFIC

OCEAN

Santa Fe ★

Arizona
(AZ)

★ Phoenix

New
Mexico
(NM)

Honolulu ★
Hawaii
(HI)
*PACIFIC
OCEAN*

| 0 | 100 | 200 Miles |
| 0 | 100 | 200 Kilometers |

North
West ★ East
South

MEXICO

| 0 | 250 | 500 Miles |
| 0 | 250 | 500 Kilometers |

CANADA

North Dakota (ND)
★ Bismarck

Minnesota (MN)
St. Paul ★

South Dakota (SD)
Pierre ★

Nebraska (NE)
Lincoln ★

Wisconsin (WI)
Madison ★

Lake Superior

Lake Michigan

Lake Huron

(MI)
Lansing ★

Lake Ontario

Lake Erie

Iowa (IA)
Des Moines ★

Illinois (IL)
Springfield ★

Indiana (IN)
Indianapolis ★

Ohio (OH)
Columbus ★

Kansas (KS)
Topeka ★

Missouri (MO)
Jefferson City ★

Kentucky (KY)
Frankfort ★

West Virginia (WV)
Charleston ★

Virginia (VA)
Richmond ★

Maine (ME)
Augusta ★

Vermont (VT)
Montpelier

New Hampshire (NH)
Concord ★

New York (NY)
Albany ★

Boston ★
Massachusetts (MA)
Providence ★
Rhode Island (RI)

Hartford ★
Connecticut (CT)

Pennsylvania (PA)
Harrisburg ★

Trenton ★
New Jersey (NJ)

Dover ★
Delaware (DE)

Annapolis ★
Maryland (MD)

Washington, D.C. ⊕

Oklahoma (OK)
Oklahoma City ★

Arkansas (AR)
Little Rock ★

Tennessee (TN)
Nashville ★

North Carolina (NC)
Raleigh ★

South Carolina (SC)
Columbia ★

Texas (TX)
Austin ★

Mississippi (MS)
Jackson ★

Alabama (AL)
Montgomery ★

Georgia (GA)
Atlanta ★

Louisiana (LA)
Baton Rouge ★

Florida (FL)
Tallahassee ★

ATLANTIC OCEAN

BAHAMAS

Gulf of Mexico

CUBA

143

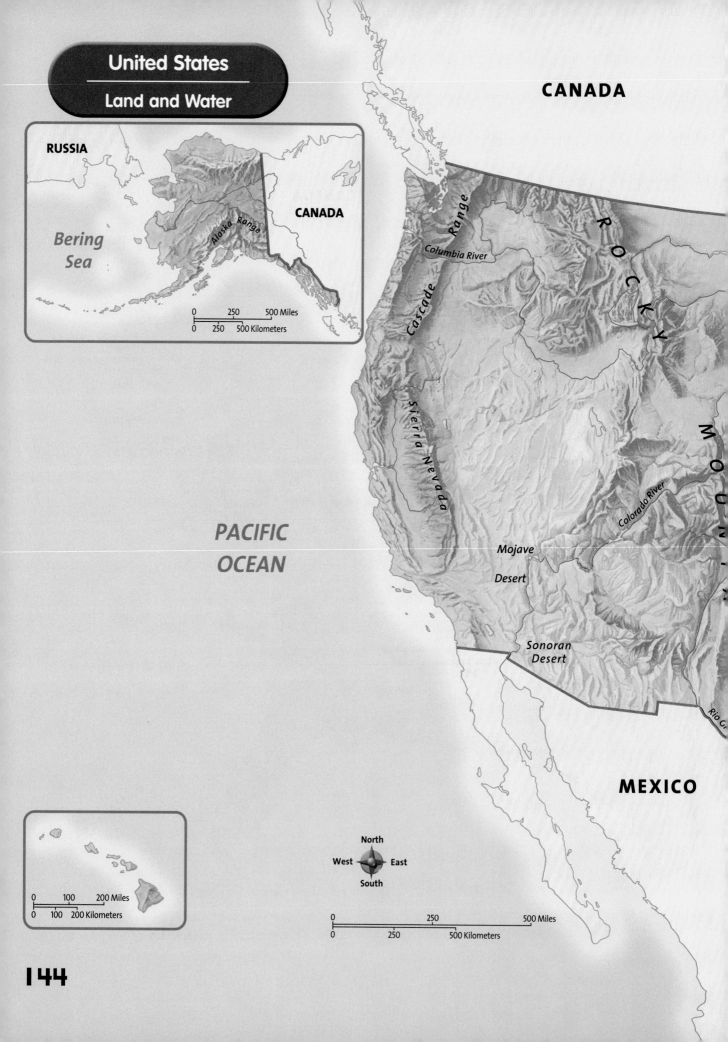

RUSSIA

CANADA

Bering
Sea

Alaska Range

CANADA

0   250   500 Miles
0   250   500 Kilometers

PACIFIC
OCEAN

Cascade Range

Columbia River

R O C K Y

Sierra Nevada

M O U N T A I

Colorado River

Mojave
Desert

Sonoran
Desert

Rio Gr

MEXICO

0   100   200 Miles
0   100   200 Kilometers

North

West   East

South

0   250   500 Miles
0   250   500 Kilometers

CANADA

Lake Superior

Lake Michigan

Lake Huron

Mississippi River

Missouri River

Lake Ontario

Lake Erie

GREAT PLAINS

INTERIOR

PLAINS

Missouri River

Ohio River

APPALACHIAN MOUNTAINS

Mississippi River

ATLANTIC
OCEAN

COASTAL PLAIN

Rio Grande

Gulf of
Mexico

BAHAMAS

Straits of Florida

CUBA

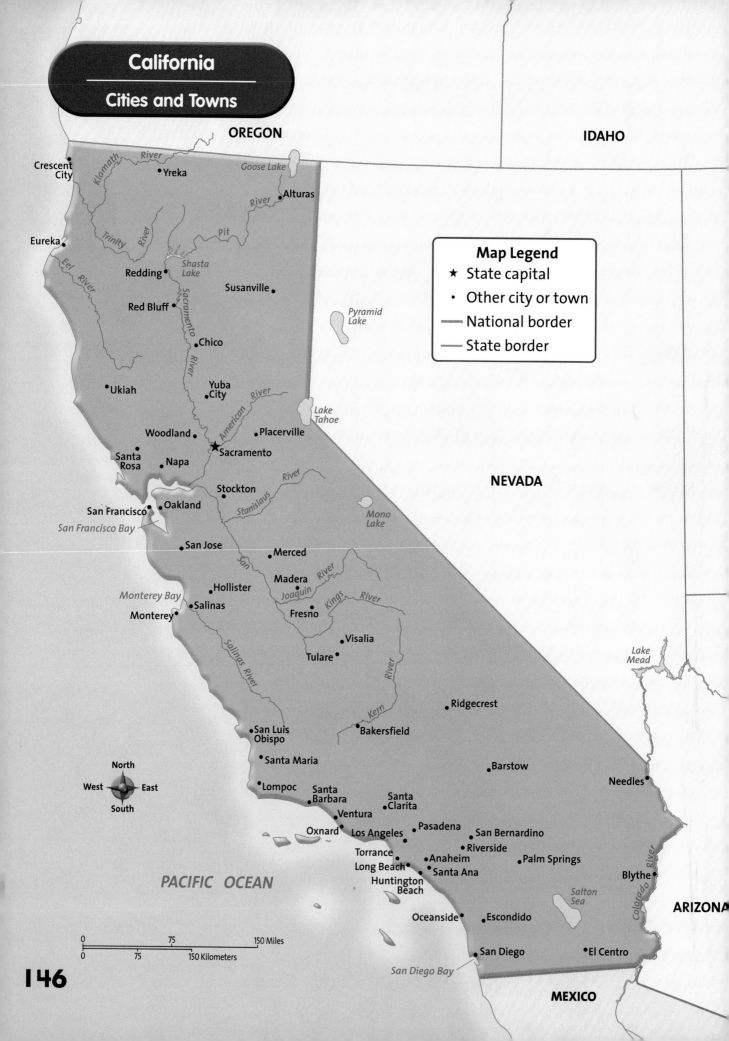

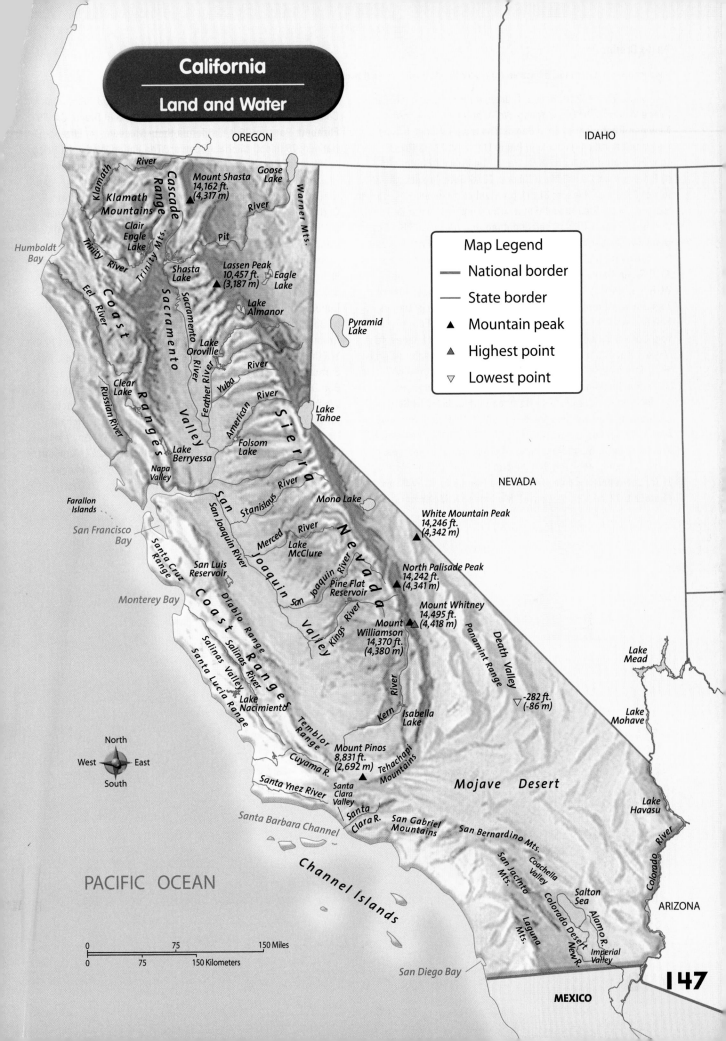

California

Land and Water

OREGON

IDAHO

Klamath River

Cascade Range

Goose Lake

Mount Shasta
14,162 ft.
(4,317 m)

Klamath Mountains

Warner Mts.

Trinity Mts.

Pit River

Clair Engle Lake

Humboldt Bay

Trinity River

Shasta Lake

Lassen Peak
10,457 ft.
(3,187 m)

Eagle Lake

Map Legend

— National border

— State border

▲ Mountain peak

▲ Highest point

▽ Lowest point

Coast Ranges

Sacramento Valley

Eel River

Lake Almanor

Sacramento River

Lake Oroville

Feather River

Pyramid Lake

Clear Lake

Russian River

Yuba River

American River

Sierra

Lake Tahoe

Lake Berryessa

Folsom Lake

Napa Valley

NEVADA

Farallon Islands

Nevada

San Joaquin River

Stanislaus River

Mono Lake

White Mountain Peak
14,246 ft.
(4,342 m)

San Francisco Bay

Santa Cruz Range

Merced River

Lake McClure

San Joaquin River

North Palisade Peak
14,242 ft.
(4,341 m)

Monterey Bay

San Luis Reservoir

Diablo Range

San Joaquin Valley

Pine Flat Reservoir

Kings River

Mount Whitney
14,495 ft.
(4,418 m)

Mount Williamson
14,370 ft.
(4,380 m)

Panamint Range

Death Valley

Lake Mead

Coast Ranges

Salinas River

Salinas Valley

Kern River

Isabella Lake

−282 ft.
(−86 m)

Lake Mohave

Santa Lucia Range

Lake Nacimiento

Temblor Range

North

West — East

South

Cuyama R.

Mount Pinos
8,831 ft.
(2,692 m)

Tehachapi Mountains

Mojave Desert

Lake Havasu

Santa Ynez River

Santa Clara Valley

Santa Clara R.

San Gabriel Mountains

San Bernardino Mts.

Colorado River

Santa Barbara Channel

PACIFIC OCEAN

Channel Islands

Coachella Valley

San Jacinto Mts.

Colorado Desert

Salton Sea

Alamo R.

ARIZONA

Laguna Mts.

New R.

Imperial Valley

0   75   150 Miles

0   75   150 Kilometers

San Diego Bay

147

MEXICO

Photo Credits